Seas & Oceans

BOOK HOUSE

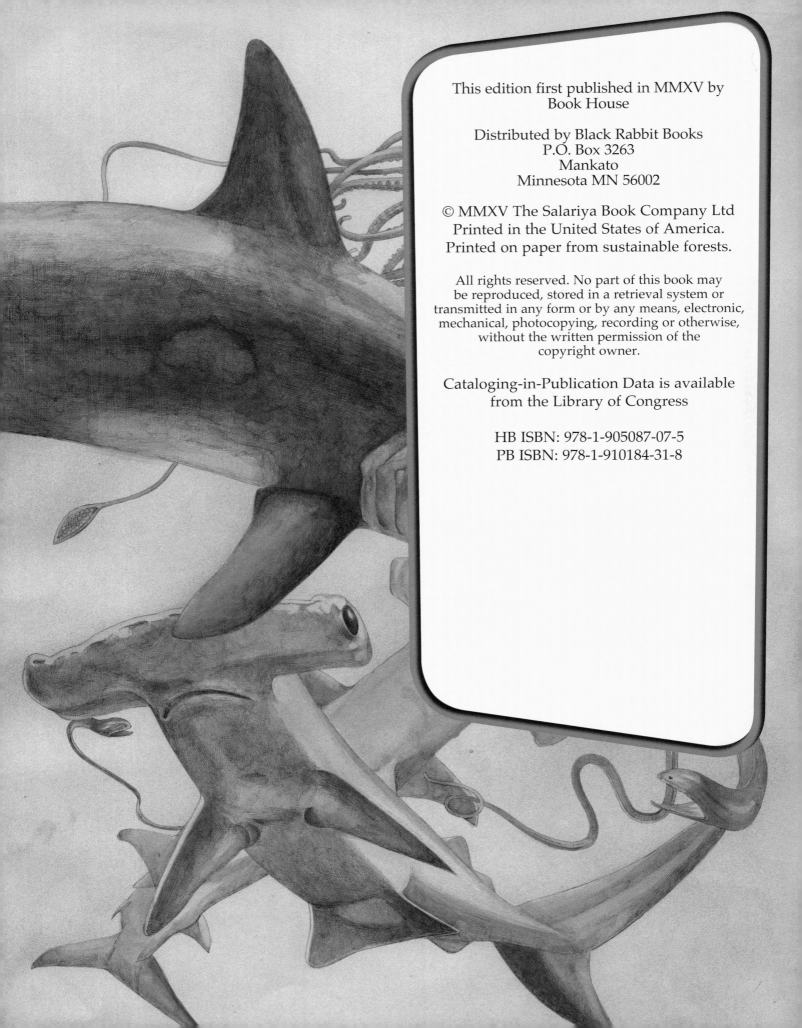

This edition first published in MMXV by
Book House

Distributed by Black Rabbit Books
P.O. Box 3263
Mankato
Minnesota MN 56002

Cataloging-in-Publication Data is available
from the Library of Congress

HB ISBN: 978-1-905087-07-5
PB ISBN: 978-1-910184-31-8

A CLOSER LOOK AT

Seas&
Oceans

Written by Margot Channing
Illustrated by Carolyn Scrace
and Mark Bergin

CONTENTS

WHAT ARE SEAS AND OCEANS?

Living on land, we easily forget that salty seawater covers most of Earth. Four enormous hollows in the planet's surface hold the waters of the Arctic, Atlantic, Indian, and Pacific oceans. The Pacific Ocean is the world's largest ocean. It is big enough to hold every continent on Earth, and its deepest part could cover the highest mountain on land!

UNDERWATER MOUNTAIN

If the oceans were drained, Earth's largest feature to be seen from space would be the mountain range that runs along the bottom of the oceans. It is more than 37,300 miles (60,000 km) long.

Mediterranean Sea

Seas and oceans hold 97 percent of the world's water and cover almost 70 percent of its surface. Large areas of partly enclosed ocean form the world's seas, such as the Mediterranean Sea.

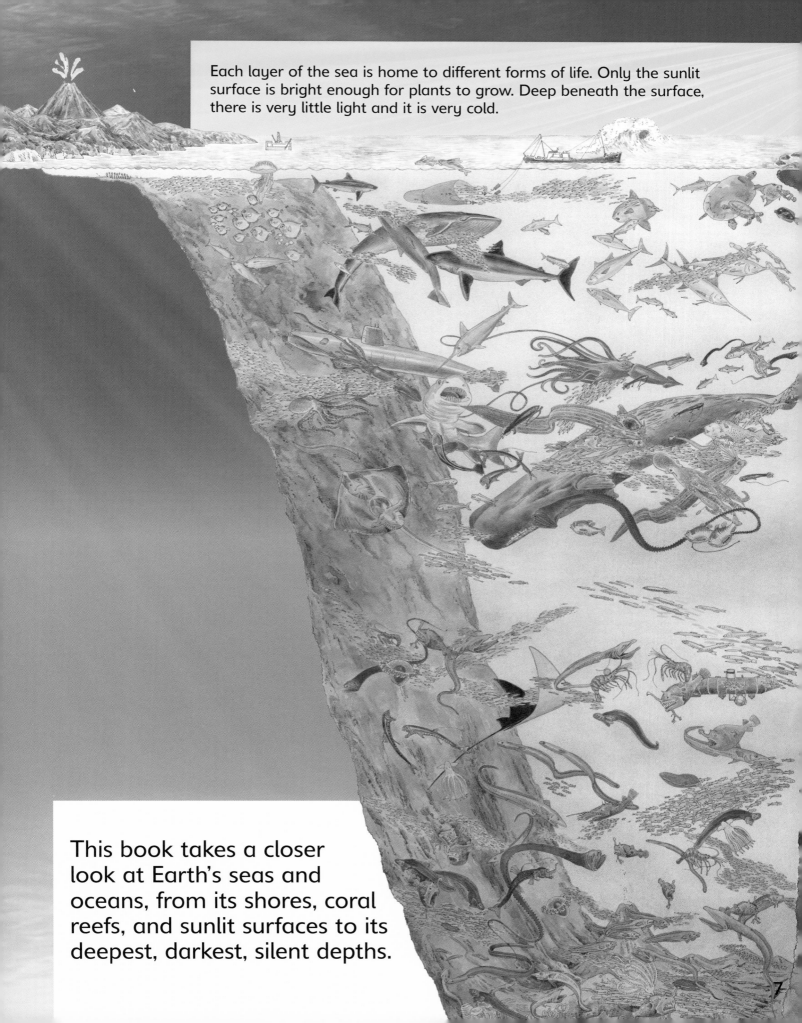

Each layer of the sea is home to different forms of life. Only the sunlit surface is bright enough for plants to grow. Deep beneath the surface, there is very little light and it is very cold.

This book takes a closer look at Earth's seas and oceans, from its shores, coral reefs, and sunlit surfaces to its deepest, darkest, silent depths.

THE SEASHORE

The seashore, where the sea meets land, is full of life. Barnacles, limpets, sea anemones, and seaweeds grip the rocky shores so tightly that even storm waves do not wrench them loose.

Herring gulls

Few creatures can hide on the shifting sandy surface of the shoreline. However, an inch or so under the surface, many animals burrow for safety.

LOW TIDE

At low tide, shellfish close their shells to keep moisture inside so their bodies don't dry up. Shore fish are stranded in little pools, and crabs squeeze under shady rocks.

HIGH TIDE

At high tide, the flooded seashore comes to life. Creatures creep out of their hiding places to feed. Burrowing animals use tubes or feelers to suck in or grab tiny pieces of food carried in by the tide. Birds prey on all these seashore creatures.

Sea anemones

Limpets

Seaweeds

Barnacles

CORAL REEFS

Coral reefs are rocklike formations that are found in the warm waters of tropical regions. A coral reef is made up of the skeletons of billions of tiny coral animals, called polyps. Each polyp attaches itself to the reef and builds up a hard, cup-shaped skeleton on the outside of its soft body. When a polyp dies, its skeleton remains, helping to build up the reef.

Coral

ALGAE AND POLYPS

Coral polyps are found only in warm, sunlit water where tiny plants called algae can grow inside the polyps' body. Algae release oxygen, which helps the polyps to breathe.

Coral grows in a variety of shapes. Some, like elkhorn, are branched. Others are rounded, like brain coral.

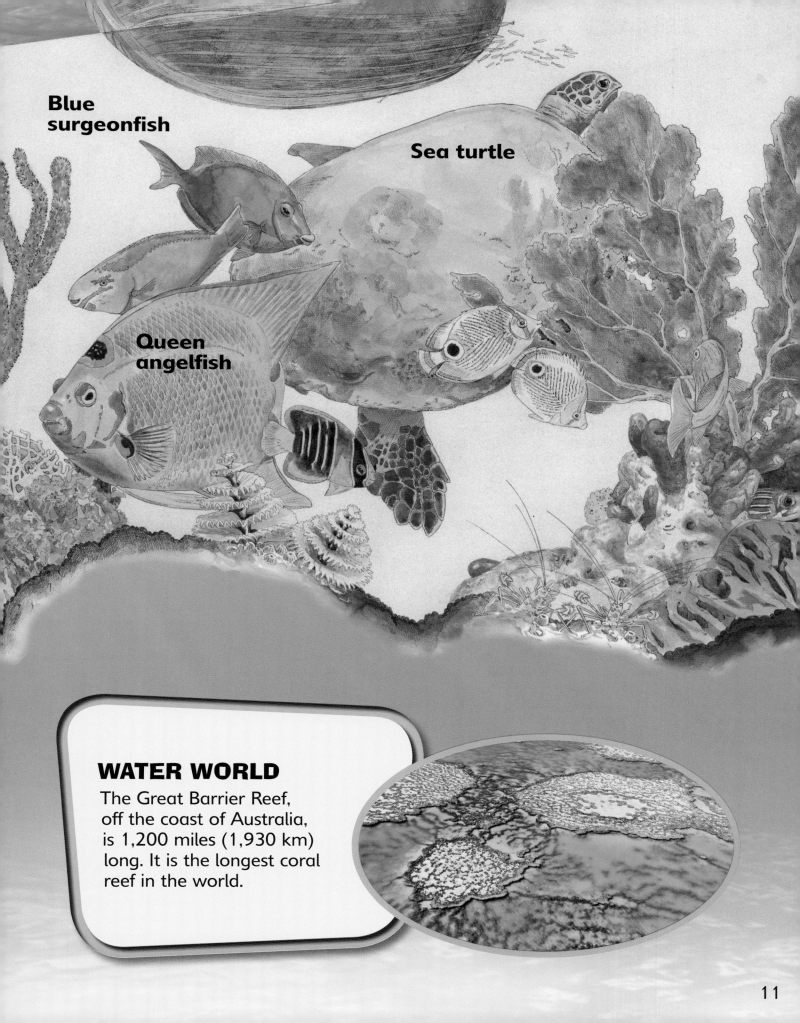

Blue surgeonfish

Sea turtle

Queen angelfish

WATER WORLD

The Great Barrier Reef, off the coast of Australia, is 1,200 miles (1,930 km) long. It is the longest coral reef in the world.

TOP OF THE OCEAN

Sunlight that is strong enough for plants to grow only reaches the top 500 ft (150 m) of the sea. This is called the "euphotic zone." Tiny drifting plants float there alongside little animals that feed on them or on one another. Together, these plants and animals form a huge living organism called "plankton."

Ocean sunfish

CONTINENTAL SHELF

The continental shelf is found in the euphotic zone. It is the seabed that surrounds Earth's continents. Many creatures live there, including eels and a huge variety of fish.

Sawfish

Sea snakes live along the continental shelf. They are venomous, or poisonous, snakes that swim in the sea.

Anchovies

Manta ray

Sea snake

PLANKTON FEEDERS

Plankton provides food for small fish such as anchovies. The anchovies then provide food for larger, fiercer hunters. Some very large animals, such as manta rays and baleen whales, feed on plankton, too.

THE MIDDLE OPEN SEA

Deep below the surface of the sea is the level known as middle open sea. This is also called the "mesopelagic zone." This level is between 500—3,300 ft (150—1,000 m) deep. It is too dark there for plants to grow. Creatures survive there by eating one another or any dead organisms that drift down from the ocean surface. Sometimes, they swim up toward the surface to feed on creatures that swim there.

Luminous prawn

Crustacean

MIDDLE SEA DEFENSE

Bonito and other small fish swim in schools for protection. Squids and jellyfish defend themselves with their deadly tentacles. Lantern fish have special chemicals that shine and sparkle like pearl buttons to help camouflage their shape.

Lantern fish

The hammerhead shark is a mesopelagic swimmer. It has a wide, flattened head that looks more like a shovel than a hammer.

Hammerhead shark

STREAMLINED HUNTERS

Sharks and many other fish that swim in the mesopelagic zone are fast-swimming hunters. They track their prey by smell or by sensing their vibrations in the water.

THE DEEP OCEAN

The deep open ocean is also known as the "bathypelagic zone." This pitch black layer is found 3,300—9,840 ft (1,000—3,000 m) below the ocean surface. At this depth, food is hard to find, so fewer creatures swim there than in the mesopelagic layer above.

FLABBY FISH

Most of the fish that swim in the bathypelagic layer have weak, flabby bodies. They ambush passing prey, rather than chasing it through the sea. The deep-sea anglerfish attracts its prey with a light that glows at the end of a "fishing rod" on top of its head!

Giant squid

Oarfish

BIG STOMACH, HUGE TEETH

The gulper fish can swallow fish much larger than itself. Its baglike stomach can expand to help it eat large creatures. The viperfish's long needlelike teeth are visible even when its mouth is closed!

Sperm whale

Gulper fish

Viperfish

Large, strong swimmers sometimes visit the bathypelagic zone. These include giant squids and ribbon-shaped oarfish, which are as long as a bus!

THE DEEP

Strange-looking fish and other creatures swim or crawl around the deepest level of the ocean. This layer is called the "abyssal zone" and is 9,840—36,100 ft (3,000—11,000 m) below the ocean surface. The water pressure at this depth is huge, and the temperature is almost freezing.

FINDING FOOD

Creatures of the abyssal zone eat dead plants and animals that sink down from the higher layers of water above.

Deep-sea anglerfish

LIVING IN THE DEEP

The most common creature in the abyssal zone is the rat tail. This fish has a long end to its tail, rather like a rat's tail.

Rat tail

Gulper fish

Abyssal octopus

Deep-sea eel

Sea snails

Brachiopods, sponges, brittle stars, and crinoids all live on the seabed of the abyssal zone.

TSUNAMIS

Tsu is Japanese for "overflowing," and *nami* means "wave." A tsunami is a giant ocean wave that overflows the land. Tsunamis are created by sudden movements of the seabed that are caused by earthquakes or volcanic eruptions.

CREATING A TSUNAMI

An underwater earthquake or a volcanic eruption can suddenly force the seabed to shift dramatically up or down. This disturbs the layers of water above the seabed. Huge ripples of water expand outward in all directions across the ocean. These are tsunamis.

Tsunami

HITTING THE SHORE

As a tsunami gets close to the shore, the waves get higher. Tsunamis have been known to rise to 60 ft (18 m) on flat, low-lying shores and to more than 100 ft (30 m) at the head of V-shaped inlets.

Tsunamis sweep inshore, smashing buildings, uprooting trees, and tossing vehicles around like tiny toys.

OIL AND GAS RIGS

Artificial islands peep above the water in parts of the North Sea, Arctic Ocean, Gulf of Mexico, and other offshore waters. These islands are the tops of oil and gas rigs that rise from the seabed.

TRANSPORTING A RIG

The steel or concrete towers of most rigs are built on land. They are then towed out to sea by tugboats and erected on the ocean floor. Many rigs stand in shallow water, but some are in water that is more than 660 ft (200 m) deep.

FIXING A RIG

Rigs are attached to the seabed by platforms. A tension leg platform is a floating platform held to the seabed by jointed legs. A steel jacket platform rests on a steel frame that is pinned to the seabed. The gravity platform sits on concrete legs that are anchored to the seabed by their great weight.

Tension leg platform

Steel jacket platform

Gravity platform

Workers and supplies are transported to and from a rig by boat or by helicopter. There are special helicopter landing pads on rigs.

Oil rig

DEEP-SEA FISHING

A modern fishing ship uses an underwater "seeing eye" called a sonar. This device shows an image of the surrounding ocean. Sonars send out sound pulses. The echo from a sound pulse changes if it encounters a shoal of fish. The signals on the ship's radar alert the captain to exactly where to fish.

FISHNETS

A trawl net is designed to catch fish at the bottom of the sea. A purse seine is drawn around a shoal of fish near the surface. It is closed with a cable so that the fish cannot escape. A beam trawl is a large net held open by a wood or metal beam.

Freezer

Trawl net

Purse seine

24

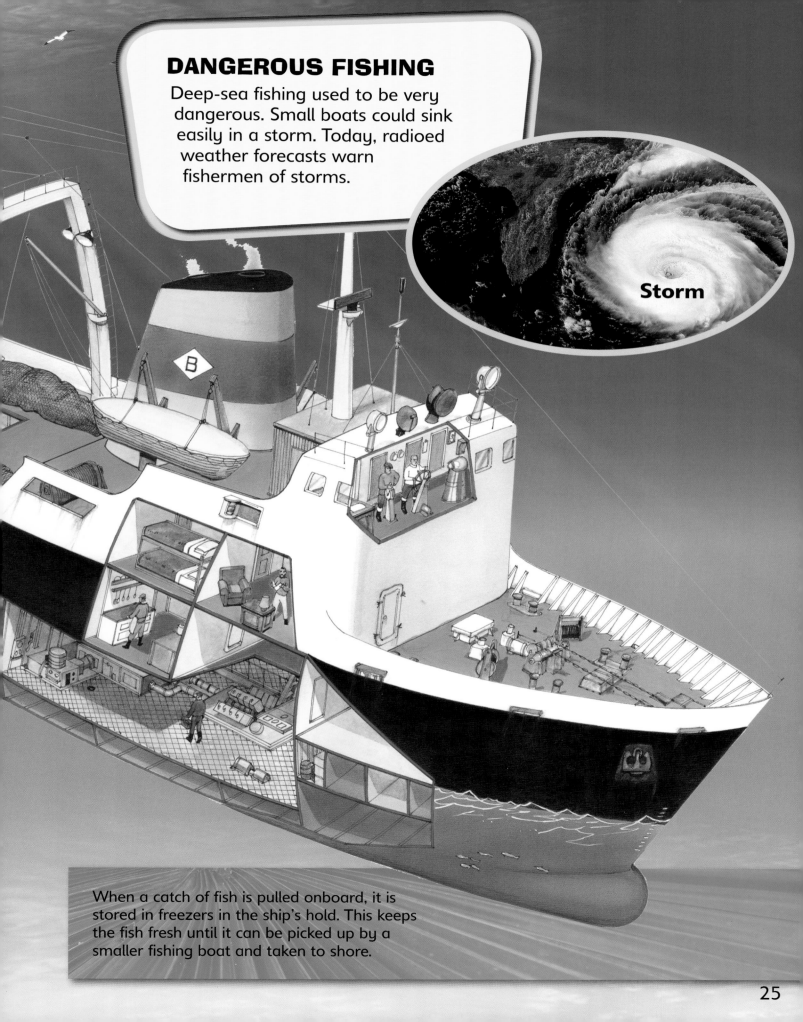

DANGEROUS FISHING

Deep-sea fishing used to be very dangerous. Small boats could sink easily in a storm. Today, radioed weather forecasts warn fishermen of storms.

Storm

When a catch of fish is pulled onboard, it is stored in freezers in the ship's hold. This keeps the fish fresh until it can be picked up by a smaller fishing boat and taken to shore.

SUBMARINES

Submarines are ships that can travel both on the sea and deep beneath its surface. When a submarine is ready to submerge, it must be made watertight. The ballast tanks are then filled with seawater until the submarine is so heavy that it sinks.

Living area

The crew works, eats, and sleeps inside the submarine.

COMING UP

To make a submarine rise, high-pressure air is blown into the ballast tanks to force out the seawater. "Wings" on the side of the submarine control how quickly it climbs.

STREAMLINED MOVING

The cigar-shaped body of a submarine is designed to move easily through the water. A propeller, powered by a very powerful engine, drives the submarine forward through the water.

EXPLORING THE OCEANS

Oceans cover 70 percent of the Earth's surface, yet, until 1960 no human had ever seen the seabed. Since then, we have made remarkable discoveries about the oceans, from deep-sea vents that shoot out boiling water, to the astonishing deep-sea creatures that live there. Who knows how many more mysteries we have yet to discover?

EARTH'S DEEPEST TRENCH

In 1960, two men named Jacques Piccard and Donald Walsh traveled almost 7 miles (11 km) below the ocean surface. In a vessel named the *Trieste*, the pair journeyed to the bottom of the Marianas Trench, the deepest trench in the world.

Trieste

Jason Junior

SUBMERSIBLE DIVING

Alvin is a research vessel that is used to discover more about the oceans. *Alvin* has a "robot" called *Jason Junior*, which is used to travel into places that are too small for *Alvin* to reach.

ALVIN

In 1985, *Alvin* provided the world's first look at the *Titanic* since its sinking in 1912.

TITANIC

GLOSSARY

Abyssal zone the pitch-black bottom layer of the ocean, from 9,840—36,100 ft (3,000—11,000 m) deep.

Algae simple plants made of one cell or chains of cells. Algae live in moist places and include seaweeds.

Baleen whales toothless whales with a fringe of baleen that hangs down from the upper jaw. The baleen traps small creatures as the whale swims along with its mouth open.

Bathypelagic zone the dark ocean layer, between 3,300—9,840 ft (1,000—3,000 m) deep.

Brittle stars spindly-armed relatives of the starfish.

Continental shelf the shallow underwater rim of the continents, averaging about 600 ft (200 m) deep.

Coral reefs rocklike formations made of the skeletons of billions of tiny sea creatures called coral polyps.

Euphotic zone the uppermost, sunlit layer of the ocean where seaweeds and other plants can grow, up to 500 ft (150 m) deep.

Gulper fish thin, deep-sea fish with an enormous mouth and a baglike stomach.

Mesopelagic layer the middle open sea, from 500—3,300 ft (150—1,000 m) deep.

Ray a type of fish with a wide, flat shape. Its skeleton is not bony but gristly like a shark's.

Shark fierce, streamlined fish with a gristly skeleton. Sharks eat other fish and some mammals, such as seals. A few species of large shark sometimes attack human swimmers.

Squid ten-armed sea creatures that are related to octopuses. A squid seizes its prey with its tentacles and then kills it with a bite. A squid quickly propels itself through the water by forcing jets of water out of its body through a narrow tube.

Viperfish a deep-sea fish with huge fangs that look similar to the fangs of a type of snake called a viper.

INDEX